D1716989

The Imaginative Explorer's Guide to the Basement

Eric Braun

BLACK
RABBIT
BOOKS

Hi Jinx is published by Black Rabbit Books
P.O. Box 3263, Mankato, Minnesota, 56002.
www.blackrabbitbooks.com
Copyright © 2021 Black Rabbit Books

Marysa Storm, editor; Michael Sellner, designer;
Omay Ayres, photo researcher

Names: Braun, Eric, 1971- author.
Title: The imaginative explorer's guide to the basement /
by Eric Braun.
Description: Mankato : Black Rabbit Books, 2021.
Series: Hi jinx. Theimaginative explorer's guide | Includes
bibliographical references.
Audience: Ages 8-12 | Audience: Grades 4-6 | Summary:
"Invites readersto take a fresh, creative look at a basement
through playful,conversational text and fun tips"–
Provided by publisher.
Identifiers: LCCN 2019026701 (print)
LCCN 2019026702 (ebook)
ISBN 9781623103262 (hardcover)
ISBN 9781644664223 (paperback)
ISBN 9781623104207 (adobe pdf)
Subjects: LCSH: Basements–Juvenile literature.
Classification: LCC NA2852 .B73 2021 (print)
LCC NA2852 (ebook) | DDC728-dc23
LC record available at https://lccn.loc.gov/2019026701
LC ebook record available at
https://lccn.loc.gov/2019026702

Printed in the United States. 1/20

Image Credits

Alamy: BNP Design Studio, Cover, 8; GL Archive, 16; Dreamstime:
19; iStock: so_illustrator, 4–5; iStock: KanKhem, 10; whitemay,
16; Shutterstock: ekler, 7; Event Horizon, 16–17; Giingerann,
9; GraphicsRF, 19; HitToon, 2–3, 21; Klara Viskova, 15; Lorelyn
Medina, 1, 2–3, 6–7, 10–11; Lyudmyla Kharlamova, 16; Memo
Angeles, 15, 18–19, 19, 20; mohinimurti, 3, 12, 21; Nazarkru,
8; NextMarsMedia, 23; Pasko Maksim, 17, 23, 24; pitju, 5, 21;
opicobello, 10–11, 13; Rawpixel.com, 20; Ron Dale, 5, 8, 12, 14,
17, 20; Ron Leishman, 18–19; vectorpouch, Cover, 1, 11; Verzzh,
12, 19; Victor Brave, Cover, 11; Every effort has been made to
contact copyright holders for material reproduced in this book.
Any omissions will be rectified in subsequent printings if notice is
given to the publisher.

Contents

Chapter 1

Dark, Dingy, and Delightful

Boy, you're bored. You've watched every unboxing video ever made. You feel like your eyes are melting right out of your head. The couch is eating you alive! You're so bored, you're counting the dust specks on the TV screen. You *need* something to do. Better turn to your imagination! There's no shortage of adventures it can lead you on.

Downstairs ... If You Dare

Why not use your imagination to check out the basement? Basements tend to gather leftover junk. Family members store things there and forget them. Basements also have creepy sounds and dark corners. It's the perfect place to use your imagination. Let's get going!

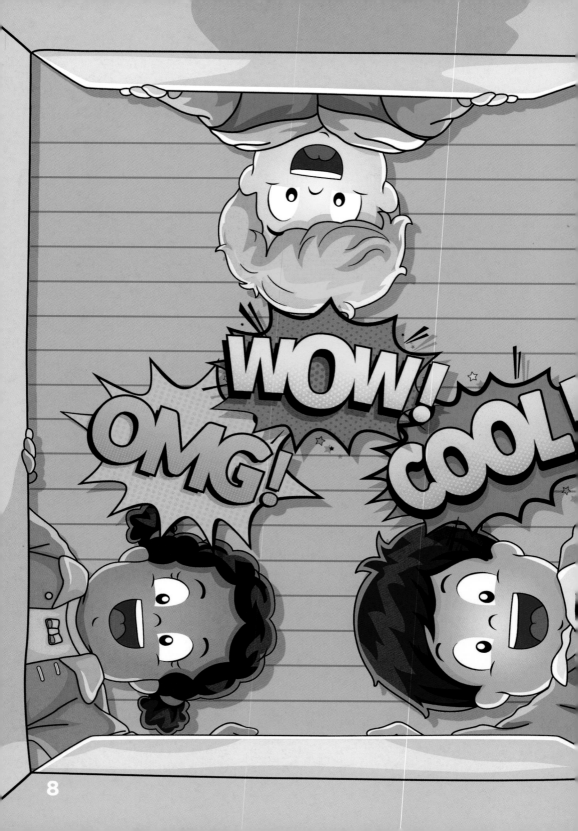

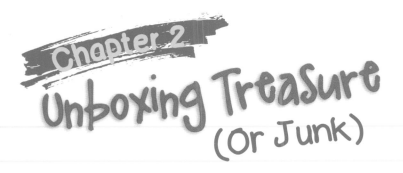

Chapter 2

Unboxing Treasure
(Or Junk)

The basement has just what you need to make your own unboxing videos. Look at all the boxes! Some are small and dusty. Others are big and dusty. Just pick one, peel back the tape, and pull open the flaps. Imagine there's a camera filming. Give it a big smile. Or scream if you find something gross. Tell your audience what you think about your discoveries.

Tip
If you have a smartphone or video camera, film yourself!

Unboxing a Whole New World

Empty boxes can be a lot of fun too. Find a nice big box. It should be one you can fit inside comfortably. Open both ends, and transform it into an airplane. If you're afraid of flying, make it a boat. Pretend you're sailing through the Bermuda Triangle!

Uses for a Cardboard Box

sailboat   robot   race car

Chapter 3
Making Friends

Believe it or not, you can make friends in the basement. Maybe you found some old clothes in those boxes. Choose a fun shirt and pants. Stuff them full of newspaper. Draw a face on a paper plate or **inflated** balloon for the head. Now you have a life-sized dummy. Say hi, and introduce yourself.

Tip

Make two or three dummies if you have enough clothes. The more the merrier, right?

Playtime

Stage a game of cards with your dummies. Put them around a table. Deal them each a hand of cards. Make it look like they've been playing for a while. You can leave the dummies for your family to find. They'll be totally creeped out!

Tip

You can also call a **sibling** or parent to the basement. Pretend you hear the dummies talking. See how they react!

YOUNG BOSTON NAT LS

taste me

E CRE

Chapter 4
Kooky Collage

The basement is a great place to get crafty! Pile up the old books and magazines. Grab the **encyclopedias** and baseball cards too. They're a **treasure trove** of images. Grab a scissors and some glue. Turn the images into trading cards. Or make an **ad** for an imaginary product you have invented.

Tip

Check with an adult before you cut anything up. Some of that stuff might be **valuable!**

Wanted!

You can also make a wanted poster. Cut out faces from magazine pages. Use part of each face to create a new one. **Paste** the new face on a piece of paper. Write "WANTED" above it in big letters. Make up a crime the person committed. Offer up a big reward for his or her capture.

Who would've guessed there was so much fun waiting below you? It just took a little imagination to discover it!

Chapter 5
Get in on the
Hi Jinx

Did you like using your imagination to make cards and ads? If so, you might want to be a graphic designer someday. They use their imaginations to combine images and words to make advertisements. They design **logos** and bring ideas to life. Maybe you'll grow up to be a graphic designer!

Take It One Step More

1. **Why do some basements seem so creepy?**

2. **You can do a lot of fun things with big basement boxes. What about smaller boxes? How could you use them to explore?**

3. **What else could you do with your dummies?**

GLOSSARY

ad (AD)—something that sells a product; ad is short for advertisement.

encyclopedia (en-sahy-kluh-PEE-dee-uh)— a book or set of books containing information on branches of learning

inflated (in-FLEYT-ed)—filled with air or another gas

logo (LO-go)—a symbol used to identify a company

paste (PEYST)—to stick on or together with a sticky mixture

sibling (SI-bling)—a brother or a sister

treasure trove (TREZH-er TROHV)— a collection of expensive or special things found in a place where it was hidden or buried

valuable (VAL-yoo-bul)—worth a lot of money

BOOKS

Braun, Eric. *The Imaginative Explorer's Guide to the Attic.* The Imaginative Explorer's Guide. Mankato, MN: Black Rabbit Books, 2021.

Devos, Sarah. *I am Never Bored: The Best Ever Craft and Activity Book for Kids: 100 Great Ideas for Kids to Do When There Is Nothing to Do.* Beverly, MA: Quarry Books, an imprint of The Quarto Group, 2018.

WEBSITES

Card Games for Kids
www.activityvillage.co.uk/card-games

Crafts & Experiments for Kids
**www.pbs.org/parents/activity-finder/ages-all/
topics-all/shows-all/types-all**

Make Your Own Trading Cards
**www.crayola.com.au/crafts/make-your-own-trading-
cards-craft/**

INDEX